I Choose You

THIS BOOK BELONGS TO

_____

Dedication

For my mother who "Chose Me" and now watches over me. To my birth mother who wanted more for me. To my loving and supportive husband who gave me the space and opportunity to go on my healing journey I can never thank you enough. To my tribe of friends your love and support means everything.

To Deb my Big Magic who helped guide me on my journey to heal!
To CJ my illustrator, coach and guide on my writing journey.
To Leanne at Red Pencil thank you for the edit
from across the world.

Words cannot express how much all of your
encouragement and belief means to me!

Thank you all!
XOXO
Megan

This book is for anyone who is adopted know you are not alone and you are always enough. To anyone who wasn't adopted always remember to be kind and see people for who they are not where they came from. You never know what someone is struggling with.

I Choose You

©2022

Author
Megan L. Shiffra

xoxo Megan

Illustrator
C.J. Jasenski

This is the story of a little girl named Meg,
she has big brown eyes and dark black hair
that she wears in pig tails on top of her
head with colorful bows.

She is adopted.

This is Lynda, Meg's adopted mom
who loves her more than anything.

Meg asks her mom all the time the story
of her, how they found each other and
how they became a family.

So, Lynda always tells her the story of the birds, Rose and Pearl. Meg loves hearing this story as it makes her feel safe, warm, and loved.

Once there was a dove
and her name was Rose.

Rose had always wanted an egg
to call her own. She had waited many years, but
she never was able to have an egg.

One day when Rose was out eating worms
and gathering nectar from the flowers,
she found a nest

She had seen this nest before as it was
beautiful but never with a bird
and now it had an egg in it.

The egg was little with light brown spots.

She watched the egg
but no bird was ever there
to look after it.

A storm was coming so
Rose decided to keep the
egg warm and safe.

Rose sat on the egg day and night for weeks.

To her surprise the egg started moving
and then hatched a little hummingbird.

Rose loved her from the start and called her
Pearl as she was so precious.

Pearl was small and looked different from her,
but Rose loved her just the same.

Rose told Pearl, "I Choose You."

Rose taught Pearl everything. She taught her
how to fly, find food, and build a nest.

As the weeks passed Pearl grew bigger
and started growing feathers. They were
multicolored and so beautiful.

Pearl was fast when she would fly.
She would whizz through the trees and flowers.

One day when Rose was out looking for worms Pearl was flying and playing with the other birds and one of them said, "You look different, you know Rose is not your mom."

Pearl flew back to the nest and told Rose what
the other birds had said to her.

Rose said, "You are different.
You are special and always remember
I choose you to be with me always and forever.
We are a family, I am your mama."

Pearl was so happy to be with Rose
and know how special she was.

A few days later Pearl went out flying,
zooming around as she was much
faster than the other birds.

She wanted to join in with the other birds
playing racing games. She was so fast
surely they would pick her.

But none of the doves picked Pearl
to be on their team. They teased
her for being different.

Pearl was very sad and went home
to tell Rose what had happened.

Rose told her again how she was different and
that's what made her special. She was chosen.
She was adopted and they were a family.

Rose told Pearl to always remember just
because something looks or acts different from
you doesn't mean there is anything wrong.

You always have a choice to do and
say what is right and be kind.

The next day Pearl was playing with the other birds and they started teasing Pearl again when one of the birds said "NO! Rose is Pearl's mama, she is special that's why Pearl looks different, they are a family."

Pearl knew she had found a true friend because she stood up for her.

Pearl knew that no matter what she was different, she was special, she was chosen and loved by Rose.

Lynda told Meg you are special and I choose you.
Just like Rose adopted Pearl, I adopted you
and we are a family.

Always remember even when I'm not with you
I choose you, yesterday, today, tomorrow
and every day after, forever and ever.

Meg was so happy she went outside
to play and pick some flowers.

Guess what... She saw the most beautiful
hummingbird with colored feathers just like
the color of the bows in her hair zooming
around the flowers drinking nectar.

Meg knew this had to be Pearl and said,
"Hello Pearl so nice to see you."

ACTIVITIES

QUESTIONS:

What story did Meg want to hear from Lynda?

What did the egg look like that Rose found?

What was special about Pearl?

What was special about Meg?

Why did Pearl go home sad?

What did Rose tell Pearl after she came home?

What did Pearl's friend do for her?

What should you do when you see someone
who is different from you?

ADOPTION INFORMATION

Around seven million Americans are adopted.

_____

It is estimated that worldwide there are
15 million children waiting for adoption.

_____

Four million babies are born in the US and
around 140,000 are adopted.

_____

One out of every 25 US families has an adopted child.

_____

Most adopted children have been teased
in school for being adopted.

Adoption Information Sources:
www.adoptioncouncil.org
www.adoption.com
www.adoptionnetwork.com

Pearl

Visit www.divinechoices.com or scan QR code
for more information and activities.

Made in the USA
Las Vegas, NV
03 December 2022